# HOW DO I KNOW IF I'M REALLY SAVED?

## JOHN ORTBERG

TYNDALE
MOMENTUM®

*The nonfiction imprint of*
*Tyndale House Publishers, Inc.*

Visit Tyndale online at www.tyndale.com.

Visit Tyndale Momentum online at www.tyndalemomentum.com.

*TYNDALE*, *Tyndale Momentum*, and Tyndale's quill logo are registered trademarks of Tyndale House Publishers, Inc. The Tyndale Momentum logo is a trademark of Tyndale House Publishers, Inc. Tyndale Momentum is the nonfiction imprint of Tyndale House Publishers, Inc., Carol Stream, Illinois.

*How Do I Know If I'm Really Saved?*

Designed by Jennifer Phelps

Edited by Jonathan Schindler

All Scripture quotations, unless otherwise indicated, are taken from the Holy Bible, *New International Version*,® *NIV.*® Copyright © 1973, 1978, 1984, 2011 by Biblica, Inc.® (Some quotations may be from the earlier NIV edition, copyright © 1984.) Used by permission. All rights reserved worldwide.

Scripture quotations marked NRSV are taken from the New Revised Standard Version Bible, copyright © 1989, Division of Christian Education of the National Council of the Churches of Christ in the United States of America. Used by permission. All rights reserved.

Scripture quotations marked NLT are taken from the *Holy Bible*, New Living Translation, copyright © 1996, 2004, 2015 by Tyndale House Foundation. Used by permission of Tyndale House Publishers, Inc., Carol Stream, Illinois 60188. All rights reserved.

For information about special discounts for bulk purchases, please contact Tyndale House Publishers at csresponse@tyndale.com, or call 1-800-323-9400.

**Library of Congress Cataloging-in-Publication Data**

Names: Ortberg, John, author.
Title: How do I know if I'm really saved? / John Ortberg.
Description: Carol Stream, Illinois : Tyndale House Publishers, Inc., [2018]
| Includes bibliographical references.
Identifiers: LCCN 2018012010 | ISBN 9781496432513 (sc)
Subjects: LCSH: Assurance (Theology) | Salvation—Christianity.
Classification: LCC BT785.O78 2018 | DDC 234—dc23 LC record available at https://lccn.loc.gov/2018012010

Printed in the United States of America

| 24 | 23 | 22 | 21 | 20 | 19 | 18 |
|----|----|----|----|----|----|----|
| 7  | 6  | 5  | 4  | 3  | 2  | 1  |

# HOW DO I KNOW IF I'M REALLY SAVED?

> We must, in fact, do nothing less than
> engage in a radical rethinking of the
> Christian conception of salvation.
>
> DALLAS WILLARD

What does it mean to be saved?

Let's face it: the world is a mess.

Hunger and poverty haven't gone away. Powerful celebrities assault women. The climate gets warmer. Marriages break up. Religion divides people. Politics can't get any uglier.

There is no question about it. Our world needs saving.

But it's not just the world. Humanity needs saving too. *I* need to be saved. Maybe so do you.

One thing is sure: if salvation is possible, it is supremely worth knowing about.

*What does it mean to be saved?*

Ours is a world where everything is at risk, and what we treasure, we long to save. We want to save rain forests and whales and Word documents. We want to save photos and letters and mementos from the important people and events in our lives. Doctors want to save limbs and lives (though mere human beings can never *really* save a life, only postpone its death).

We have savings accounts because we value money. We mark daylight saving time on the calendar because we value hours and minutes and seconds. Politicians promise to save jobs, or culture, or a way of life—or even to save us from war.

Even in our games, we seek salvation. Relief pitchers "save" a win. Goalies who stop the other team from scoring record a "save."

Movies like *Saving Private Ryan* remind us that the saving of a human life is a drama like no other, and in that particular story, the sacrifice of one life for another touches us in a way no other story can.

*But what does it* mean *to be saved?*

We long for salvation. And yet it is a word that has lost much of its urgency, especially in the world familiar with Christianity, simply because we *think* we know what it means.

The truth is, it has become trivialized, formulaic, and disconnected from daily life.

The phrase *paradigm shift* is much over-used, but I believe something like it is needed here. Salvation is too important a word to languish in misunderstanding.

My good friend Dallas Willard once wrote, "We must, in fact, do nothing less than engage in a radical rethinking of the Christian conception of salvation."[1]

I think he's right.

Somewhere along the way, the power and the promise of the gospel has been lost. We've shrunk it down, and in doing so, we've shrunk God down. The salvation that Jesus came to offer is bigger and grander and more vital than what we have turned it into.

It is the hope of the world.

It is the reclamation of human life.

It is the promise of meaning.

It provides the security to live at peace each day, to face the past without guilt and the future without fear.

That is why "we must . . . do nothing less than engage in a radical rethinking of the Christian conception of salvation."

This little booklet contrasts two ways of thinking about the term *salvation*.

The first revolves around how people can be sure they'll go to heaven when they die, and it usually involves affirming certain beliefs or praying a particular prayer that results in making one a "Christian."

The other is about experiencing eternal life under God's reign and power right now. It's less about relocation than about transformation. It's less about what God wants to do *to* you and more about what God wants to do *in* you. It's not about getting into heaven; it's about heaven getting into you.

I believe the latter version is the correct one, the one Jesus taught, the one that changed history.

*So what does it mean to be saved?*

I'll give my best, short, clear answer to the title question "How do I know if I'm really saved?" at the end of this little booklet.

But first, we have to start here:

## What Salvation Isn't

Before we talk about what salvation *is*, we need to talk about what salvation is not.

There is an old story about two students from a Christian college who were going door-to-door sharing their faith. One of the doors was answered by a harried mother carrying an infant in one arm and operating a vacuum cleaner with the other. The students could hear a baby crying in the background and see a toddler scribbling on the walls with a crayon, a pot boiling over on the stove, and a pile of dirty laundry in the corner.

"Ma'am, are you interested in eternal life?" they asked.

Utterly frazzled, the mother heaved an exasperated sigh and lamented, "Frankly, I don't think I could stand it."

Now, provided the door wasn't abruptly slammed in their faces, odds are those students would have shared the gospel with her. Why? Because for many people—Christians in particular—the gospel is the divine arrangement that, once heard and accepted, ensures the person a place in heaven.

In other words, if you believe the right things—that Jesus is the Son of God and that he died on the cross to forgive your sins—you will be allowed into heaven when you die.

It reminds me of the climax of the movie *Monty Python and the Holy Grail*, when King Arthur and his knights come to the castle they've been seeking. Lying between them and the castle is a bottomless abyss, and a wizened old bridge keeper guards the only bridge that allows access. If they can give the correct answers to his questions, they are allowed to cross. If not, they are cast into the abyss.

I think this is how many people today think about salvation. When we die, we are either headed for the castle (heaven) or the abyss (hell), and "salvation" is knowing the right answers so that God has to allow us to cross the bridge.

The problem is, Jesus doesn't talk about salvation that way. Jesus never said, "Believe the right things about me and I'll let you into heaven after you die."

In fact, Jesus—and the entire New Testament, for that matter—defines "eternal life" only once, with great precision, and in a way that has been largely lost in our day. Jesus says, "This is eternal life, that they may know you, the only true God, and Jesus Christ whom you have sent" (John 17:3, NRSV).

In other words, Eternal Life = Knowing God.

Notice Jesus doesn't say, "That they may

know *about* you." He says, "That they may *know* you."

What's the difference?

A lot of people know *about* God. Even atheists know *about* God. But *knowing* God, as Jesus speaks of it, is something wholly different. Knowing God means to know myself as his beloved friend as a gift of grace. Knowing God is to live in a rich, moment-by-moment, interactive, participatory life together. Knowing God means to experience what Paul called "the power of his resurrection" (Philippians 3:10) in the details and tasks and challenges of our daily, ordinary lives.

Knowing God means awakening to the reality that within each and every moment of our lives is an opportunity to walk with God, to talk to God, to enjoy God, to depend on God, to thank God, to need God, to serve God, and to rest in God.

And the best part is he's already here. We

just have to show up and spend time with him.

When you need help, tell him. Then pay attention and look for him to give you the strength or wisdom or the right idea you need to keep moving forward. When you are joyful, recognize his goodness behind the joy and take time to praise him. When you see beauty, recognize the hand of the Artist and thank him. Ask him to open your eyes even more so that you can see the world from his perspective. Ask God to share his experiences with you. Say, "Father, what do you feel when you look at this person? What was in your heart when you created this tree? How much joy do you experience when you look at the vast beauty of what you've created?"

People who are intentional about being connected with God have a way of finding him in the unlikeliest places. St. Ignatius spoke of finding God in all things.

Missionary Frank Laubach called it playing the "game with minutes," in which the goal was to "bring God to mind at least one second out of every sixty."[2] Brother Lawrence, a seventeenth-century Carmelite monk, described it like this:

> During my work, I would always continue to speak to the Lord as though He were right with me, offering Him my services and thanking Him for His assistance. Also, at the end of my work, I used to examine it carefully. If I found good in it, I thanked God. If I noticed faults, I asked His forgiveness without being discouraged, and then went on with my work, still dwelling in Him.[3]

*This* is eternal life.

It's not the procurement of an insurance policy that doesn't kick in until after you die, nor is it a magical "get out of jail free" card that ensures us a place in heaven someday. It's not about knowing the right answers or affirming the right doctrine in church.

It's the unspeakably rich, interactive fellowship and joy that exists between Father, Son, and Holy Spirit.

It's about knowing God—awakening to his extraordinary presence in the midst of your ordinary days, removing the obstacles that keep you from having an intimate relationship with him, seeing the world and all of humanity through his eyes, and abiding in his love and protection.

It's about allowing Jesus' life to permeate our lives one choice, one moment, and one heartbeat at a time.

*This* is what it means to be saved.

## I Thought All I Had to Do Was Say "the Prayer"?

One of the other popular misconceptions about salvation is that all you have to do is recite the Sinner's Prayer and you will be saved. One problem with this idea (and there are several) is this: the prayer doesn't appear anywhere in the Bible. Trust me—I've checked.

Another problem is that many people find that after they pray the magic prayer, they don't feel the dramatic inner change they expected to experience. They wonder if they did it right. So they pray the prayer again the next night, the next week, the next year. They're troubled that perhaps they're not really "in."

The problem is not that they said the prayer incorrectly. The problem is that their definition of salvation is too small. The problem is that they're defining salvation as having their entrance application to heaven accepted rather than receiving life from Jesus from one moment to the next.

The biggest problem is that, in this view, salvation becomes the minimum amount you have to believe such that, if you believe it, God has to let you into heaven.

Imagine Jesus himself teaching this. Imagine that Jesus said, "Believing my teaching is true—that's optional. Believing I can run your life—and allowing me to do so—that's optional. As long as you believe that my death paid for your sins, you don't need to worry about doing what I said insofar as heaven is concerned."

Or imagine him tacking a "salvation caveat" onto the Sermon on the Mount: "Everyone who hears these words of mine and puts them into practice is like a wise man who built his house on the rock. But everyone who hears these words of mine and does not put them into practice is like a foolish man who built his house on sand. But just to be clear—you don't have to worry about actually doing anything I say as long as you believe my death pays for your sins."

It is unimaginable that Jesus would be thinking this way. Saving faith is that faith which allows us to engage in interactive, grace-powered life with him beginning here and now, which death will be powerless to interrupt.

Let's consider another, more temporal example.

Let's say I acquire elite status in an airline's frequent flyer program and I ask, "What's the bare minimum I have to do to maintain my status?" This is an altogether proper question, because there is no connection between the perks I desire and the person I'm becoming. Anyone would want better seats, nicer food, linen napkins, red carpets. It is an objective, forensic, legal status. The airline will even help me keep track of my miles to make sure I can satisfy the minimum requirements.

But imagine I had said to my wife, Nancy, on our wedding day, "I want to know: What's the absolute least I can do to be married to you? What's the lowest level of commitment, the fewest affirmations, the smallest promises, the highest level of ignorance permissible— what are the minimum requirements for maintaining my husband status?"

It would have been a very short ceremony.

Marriage is not just a legal status. It is a personal, spiritual, relational reality where the relationship itself is the perk. Not just anybody wants to be married. It requires desiring fidelity, being severely limited in choosing sexual partners, being vulnerable, serving the other, being committed, giving up the remote control.

Are there minimum requirements for remaining married? For sure. Marriages end every day, but the minimum requirements are not fully knowable in advance. They depend upon the heart. If you really want the marriage, the minimum requirements will take care of themselves. And if you don't really want the marriage, the minimum requirements won't matter.

The Bible often compares salvation to marriage but never to airline status.

Trust me—I've checked.

## Doesn't Ephesians 2:8 Say That We Are Saved by Grace?

Of course we are saved by grace. We have to be. Why? Because without God's grace, we're basically a mess.

In fact, you can divide the mess that is our lives into two categories: external problems and internal ones. External problems involve things like money, possessions, careers, health, and relationships. Internal problems include things like ego, addiction, insatiable desire, envy, coldheartedness, and deceit.

Salvation as described in the Bible is about being rescued from the whole chaotic mess that is our existence. There is no category of human need that God doesn't want to redeem. But it's our internal disorder that the biblical writers say is our deepest problem.

Salvation doesn't mean simply being rescued from the consequences of our wrong choices. It doesn't mean being delivered into better circumstances. It means being changed. Salvation isn't primarily a matter of going to the good place when we die but of becoming a good person.

We are saved inwardly from our anger, despair, lust, greed, arrogance, and egotism. If our inner person is not transformed, our outer location won't matter much.

This inner transformation—the means by

which we are delivered from our addiction to sin—is what being "saved by grace" is all about. All the gifts of energy and life we're given are gifts of grace.

Eternal life is nothing you can earn. It is a free gift. But growing into it is a vital, active thing. As Dallas Willard used to say, "Grace is not opposed to *effort*, but is opposed to *earning*."[4]

Biblical salvation is so much more than having satisfied the minimum requirements; it is the grace-powered redemption of our thoughts and desires and wills and actions into cosmic meaning and divine love that leads us ever onward and upward.

Here's an analogy that might help. In Alcoholics Anonymous, the twelfth and final step speaks of someone having had a "spiritual awakening":

When a man or a woman has a spiritual awakening, the most

important meaning of it is that he has now become able to do, feel, and believe that which he could not do before on his unaided strength and resources alone. He has been granted a gift which amounts to a new state of consciousness and being. He has been set on a path which tells him he is really going somewhere, that life is not a dead end, not something to be endured or mastered. In a very real sense he has been transformed.[5]

Salvation works the same way. Paul writes:

Wake up, sleeper,
rise from the dead,
and Christ will shine on you.

EPHESIANS 5:14

It's not just that we get to see his light. His life awakens us to a new possibility for our lives. When we hit bottom, we see both the reality of our character defects and the possibility of a new life with him.

With this spiritual awakening comes the possibility of not just seeing Christ's light but becoming a part of it:

> You are the light of the world. . . .
> Let your light shine before others,
> that they may see your good deeds
> and glorify your Father in heaven.
> MATTHEW 5:14-16

Notice that Jesus doesn't say, "Try harder to make your light shine." Lamps don't have to try hard. They glow based on what's going on inside them.

This is where most people get God wrong. Most people think, *God's up there, and in addition to all the other stuff I have to do every day, I have to do things to keep God happy.*

But in John 15:5 Jesus says, "I am the vine; you are the branches. If you remain in me and I in you, you will bear much fruit; apart from me you can do nothing."

We are the branch, and the branch's job is not to produce fruit. The branch's job is simply to learn to continually receive life from the vine (God). The fruit is a natural by-product of remaining in him.

Your light will never shine brighter by trying to shine brighter. You will never produce the right fruit by trying to produce the right fruit. You will never say and do the right thing by trying to say and do the right thing. You will never obey the law by trying to obey the law. You will never do the right actions by trying to do the right actions.

That is what Paul meant when he wrote, "Continue to work out your salvation with fear and trembling, for it is God who works in you to will and to act according to his good purpose" (Philippians 2:12-13).

In fact, too often people restrict the meaning of *grace* to just the forgiveness of sins. But God was gracious before anyone sinned. We experience grace primarily as God's power in us to do what we could not do on our own. Peter said we are to "grow in grace" (see 2 Peter 3:18). That doesn't mean that we should "grow in the forgiveness of our sins"; rather, it means we should grow in our ability to rely on God's power for a life of love and joyful servanthood.

People inside the church often feel victimized by a bait-and-switch approach to spiritual life. First, they're told that in order to become a Christian or to get saved they have to do absolutely nothing.

Sometimes salvation will even be defined with the words *do* and *done*, the idea being that other religions tell you to do something, but in Christianity, salvation is done for you. People are assured they don't have to do anything to be saved.

Then, when they come back to church the next week, they're told to start *doing* things: give to the poor; care for the sick and the elderly; give time, money, and possessions freely and without hesitation. Sometimes they're told they should do this out of gratitude for being forgiven, which creates the illusion that obedience is something we do for God's sake rather than because it is the way of life for someone who follows Jesus.

There is nothing we can do to *earn* God's love. However, salvation that does not transform our "doings" would be no salvation at all.

We are not called to try harder to do good works that we don't want to do. We are called to live in union with Jesus in such a way that good works flow naturally out of our transformed inner life.

We are called to follow him.

We are called to be disciples.

## Does This Mean That It's Not Enough to Be a "Christian" and That I Have to Be a "Disciple" in Order to Be Saved?

That depends on what someone means by the word *Christian*.

According to Brad Wright, a sociologist at the University of Connecticut, a Christian is usually defined as someone who holds to certain doctrinal beliefs or who affiliates with a particular denomination or church.

Others' definitions are slightly more toxic. To paraphrase pastor and writer Andy Stanley, many people define Christians as moralistic, homophobic, anti-science, judgmental bigots who don't believe in dinosaurs but do believe they are the only ones going to heaven and secretly relish the idea that everyone else is going to hell.

Interesting enough, for many historians, a test case for defining Christianity involves Abraham Lincoln. In fact, historians have been debating whether or not Lincoln was a Christian since the late 1800s.

In Michael Burkhimer's book on the subject, he notes that before you can decide about Lincoln you must first confront "the essential question of what it means to be a Christian." He also notes that most writers and historians use three central beliefs as a criteria:

- that Jesus Christ was divine and part of a Trinity,
- that Christ died for the sins of the world, and

- that faith in this doctrine is necessary for one to gain salvation.

While he acknowledges this simplifies the matter, he nonetheless notes, "it is a foundation almost all are familiar with."[6]

But do you know where the term *Christian* is never defined? The Bible. Literally. The Bible never defines the word *Christian*. It never calls anyone to become a Christian, and it never records anyone becoming a Christian.

Jesus never uses the word *Christian* either. Jesus never says, "Here's how to become a Christian." Jesus never describes what a Christian is. Jesus himself wasn't a Christian; he was Jewish.

Jesus didn't tell his friends, "Go into all the world and make Christians."

But he did tell them to go into the world and make *disciples*.

In fact, the Bible uses the word *disciple* 269 times. *Christian*, on the other hand, only comes up three times—and that was only because Jesus' followers were becoming too ethnically diverse to be regarded as a sect within Judaism.

As Dallas Willard wrote in *The Spirit of the Disciplines*, "The New Testament is a book about disciples, by disciples, and for disciples."[7]

So how, then, is a "disciple" different from a "Christian"?

For many people—inside the church and out—Christians are thought of as people who believe the gospel of the minimum entrance requirements, who are saved because they believe the right things, which means they will be allowed into heaven when they die.

The gospel of the minimum entrance requirements is what Dietrich Bonhoeffer calls "cheap grace":

The upshot of [cheap grace] is that my only duty as a Christian is to leave the world for an hour or so on a Sunday morning and go to church to be assured that my sins are all forgiven. I need no longer try to follow Christ, for cheap grace, the bitterest foe of discipleship, which true discipleship must loathe and detest, has freed me from that.[8]

But we now know that Jesus never said, "Believe the right things about me, and I'll let you into heaven after you die." His news was something far grander, more cosmic, more life-changing, more costly, more compelling, and more humbling than that.

To the contrary, Jesus' Good News is that eternal life—life with God and for God, life under God's care, and life by God's power—is available now. If you want that life, the logical step is to become a disciple—an *apprentice*—of Jesus.

An apprentice is someone who commits to be with a master craftsman and to learn from the craftsman how to master the craft. In fact, the word for disciple in the New Testament was often used for trade apprenticeship. It's not a special church word for the spiritual elite; anyone can do it.

It's not about the skill of the apprentice; it's about the power of the Master.

Simon Sinek gave a famous TED talk where he described what he calls "the golden circle."[9] Any company, movement, or cause, he said, will have three concentric circles. The outer circle is the "what"—here's what we make or do. Inside that is a smaller circle, the "how"—here's how we do it.

As a general rule, in the life of organizations, everybody will know what the "what" is. And most people will know what the "how" is. But very few will know what's in the third circle, the innermost circle—the golden circle. That circle contains the "why."

The church's "what" is to make disciples, or apprentices. The "how" is by learning to be with Jesus and by learning from Jesus how to live like Jesus. We do this through spiritual practices, through experiences like suffering, and through the guidance of the Holy Spirit.

That leads to the "why."

Dallas Willard defines the "why" like this: "There is no problem in human life that apprenticeship to Jesus cannot solve."

You name the problem—greed, fear, racism, injustice, divorce, sexual assault, neglect, pollution, suffering, addiction, rejection, bitterness, violence, apathy, grief, war, death.

Human problems will not be solved by human means.

Human problems will not be solved by human nature.

Human nature is our biggest problem.

There are many problems technology will never solve.

There are many problems education will never solve.

There are many problems money will never solve.

There are many problems religion will never solve.

But there is no problem in human life that apprenticeship to Jesus cannot solve. That includes the forgiveness of our sins and the promise of life with God forever after death, but it also includes every other part of our existence, starting with here and now.

This is why Dietrich Bonhoeffer wrote, "Grace and discipleship are inseparable. . . . Happy are they who know that discipleship simply means the life which springs from grace, and that grace simply means discipleship."[10]

Jesus' gospel is the offer of life as an apprentice of Jesus, by grace, through faith, in this world and the world to come. It is the greatest invitation ever given to human beings. Because there is no problem in human life that apprenticeship to Jesus cannot solve.

## How Do I Become a Disciple?

I'll let Jesus answer that one: "Whoever wants to be my disciple must deny themselves and take up their cross daily and follow me" (Luke 9:23).

"Follow me." That may be the greatest and most life-changing invitation ever uttered.

You'll notice Jesus didn't say, "Obey me" (although, of course, obedience is part of following him). He didn't say, "Believe the right stuff about me" (although believing that Jesus was right—about everything—is part of following him). He didn't say, "Serve me" (although, ultimately, that is our greatest purpose). He simply asks us to go for a walk. That seems simple enough. In fact, Jesus walked so much that "walking with Jesus" became a common way of describing discipleship in the New Testament.

To love Jesus meant to walk with him. It still does.

For many centuries, the oldest way of describing that walk involved certain stages—dynamics that describe the way God works in our lives.

The first stage is called awakening, which essentially means becoming aware of God's extraordinary presence every day. The best way I can describe this is with a picture book that my kids used to like when they were little. The book was called *Where's Waldo?*, and on every page, there was this character named Waldo hidden somewhere in the background of a ridiculously busy scene. As the book went on, he got increasingly harder to find.

Now, just as "Waldo identification" is a learned skill, so too is the ability to recognize God in any given situation. Sometimes he's hard to miss; sometimes he's easy to miss. But he's always there. And recognizing God's presence and asking, "What are you calling me to do right now?" is what it means to awaken to him.

The second stage is called purgation. This stage involves identifying all the things you do that keep God at arm's length, confessing them, asking God to remove them, and engaging in practices that help free you from them.

Maybe you are obsessed by your need to be successful. Maybe you lie so often that you don't even notice anymore. Maybe you've grown deeply cynical, constantly judging others. Or perhaps you live with chronic jealousy and harbor resentment toward people with happy marriages or whose kids are flourishing or who have more successful careers than you.

Purgation is about freedom. When we confess our sins to Jesus and ask him to help us overcome them, appetites that were once our master take their rightful place as servants, leaving us free to think and focus our attention on God.

The third stage is called illumination. Illumination is a clumsy word for the process by which we come to see and think differently. Jesus' mental map becomes our mental map, and we begin to see the world as he sees it.

I don't know of a better picture of illumination than from the autobiography of Helen Keller:

> We walked down the path to the well-house. . . . Some one was drawing water and my teacher placed my hand

under the spout. As the cool stream gushed over one hand she spelled into the other the word water, first slowly, then rapidly.

I stood still, my whole attention fixed upon the motions of her fingers. Suddenly I felt a misty consciousness as of something forgotten—a thrill of returning thought; and somehow the mystery of language was revealed to me.

I knew then that "w-a-t-e-r" meant the wonderful cool something that was flowing over my hand. That living word awakened my soul, gave it light, hope, joy, set it free! . . .

I left the well-house eager to learn. Everything had a name, and each name gave birth to a new thought. As we returned to the house every object which I touched seemed

to quiver with life. That was because
I saw everything with the strange,
new sight that had come to me.[11]

She had been alone, and now she was not.
She had been imprisoned in her mind, and
now she was set free. She had felt useless,
and now she had a great purpose that would
inspire millions. Her world blossomed, and
she along with it.

"That living word awakened my soul,
gave it light, hope, joy, set it free!"

This is illumination.

The final stage is called union. In this
stage, we begin to experience the life that
Jesus described when he said, "Abide in me
as I abide in you" (John 15:4, NRSV).

His presence becomes a reality and not
just an idea. That means he can communi-
cate thoughts to me at any moment. It means
he is present to my will, and I can surrender

to him all day long. Union with Christ means I cease to identify with my old, false, hidden self and identify with the life of Jesus.

Now, it is important to realize that these four stages—awakening, purgation, illumination, and union—are not a linear process. Progressing through them is not like being a baby and then a child and then an adolescent and then an adult, where when you enter a new stage, you are entirely done with the old one. These stages are much more like the seasons of a year or the twelve steps in Alcoholics Anonymous in that we are never truly done with any of them but rather are continually involved in learning and relearning.

Thomas Merton said about prayer, "We do not want to be beginners [at prayer]. But let us be convinced of the fact that we will never be anything but beginners, all our life!"[12]

This is true, not just about prayer, but about the whole of the spiritual life.

The goal of the spiritual life is not to "get through" the stages. It is simply to continue taking one small step after another on our great journey with God.

"Take up your cross daily and follow me."

That's what discipleship is all about.

## How Can We Tell Who Is a Disciple and Who Isn't?

One of our great desires in life is to know who is "in" and who is "out" of our particular group, especially when it comes to questions like "Who is a Christian and who isn't?"

Unfortunately, many Christians today harbor a reputation of exclusivity when it comes to those who don't affirm the same set of beliefs they do.

One of the most striking aspects of Jesus' approach, however, was the way in which he treated those in the "out" group. He was strangely welcoming to the types of people who were normally shunned, and he made pronouncements about who was "in" that shocked and bewildered those around him.

In fact, what got Jesus into more trouble than anything else is that he often warned people who were *sure* they were insiders—the religious leaders and Pharisees—that they were in danger of being outside, and he treated people everyone *knew* were outsiders—Samaritans, lepers, tax collectors, prostitutes, and divorcées—as though they might actually be "in."

His goal wasn't to keep people out; it was to draw people in. He didn't focus on boundaries; he focused on the center.

An old teacher of mine, Paul Hiebert, wrote an article once that might be helpful here. He wrote that there are essentially two ways of identifying things.[13] One is called a "bounded set." With bounded sets, the way you determine whether an object is in or out is by carefully defining the boundary and measuring everything against it.

For instance, you could determine whether or not something is a triangle by saying that it must meet the minimum requirements of being a geometric shape that has exactly three distinct sides and three distinct angles. A circle, for example, will never be a triangle. It cannot become more triangle-y. And a triangle cannot become square-ish. The object either satisfies the criteria or it doesn't. It's static.

The other is called a "centered set." Here objects are defined not by the boundary but by their orientation to the center. This group is more dynamic and allows for movement over time.

For example, if we were trying to define "bald people," the person at the absolute center would be someone like Mr. Clean, while someone like Albert Einstein would be about as far from the center as you can get. Now, a baby may be born bald—and so is in the group—but as the baby begins to grow hair, he or she moves farther out. On the other hand, a twenty-year-old may have a full head of hair, but as it begins to recede, he moves closer to the center. But both are still part of the group. What's the number of hairs *required* for membership? Only God—who has literally numbered the hairs on your head—knows for sure.

If we think of Christianity as a bounded set, we will focus on the boundary. We will want to define what the necessary and sufficient conditions are for being in. Maybe it's that someone checked "Christian" as their preferred religion on a survey, or prayed the Sinner's Prayer, or professed a belief that Jesus is divine.

If Christianity is a bounded set, then we

will want to be very clear about what the necessary and sufficient conditions are to get people inside. Our goal will be to get people to cross the boundary from outside to inside. Once they're in, any further progress is optional. We can turn our attention to others who we believe have not yet crossed the boundary.

If Christianity is a bounded set, we will tend to focus on those issues that differentiate who is in and who is out, rather than those issues that were central to Jesus' primary concern. Membership in the group is static. You either are a member or you aren't, and your status is defined solely by the minimum requirements determined by some outside authority—usually the church or other Christians.

However, the New Testament presents a community of disciples that looks much more like a centered set than a bounded set.

The center, of course, is Jesus. He defines and incarnates life in the Kingdom of God and makes it available to others. This life is a call to love God with all that you are and to love your neighbor as yourself.

If we view Christianity as a centered set, then we will want to constantly orient ourselves toward God and his will and his love. We will want to be ever moving toward it. We will want to invite and help other people to be ever moving toward it. What matters is the orientation and posture of our lives. We are not worried about who is "us" and who is "them." We know that God knows, and that is enough for us. We trust him to do right by each person, including those we love most.

This is why having a centered approach to Jesus is so helpful; it reminds us that following Jesus is not a static religious identity but a dynamic calling that constantly invigorates and challenges us.

C. S. Lewis once wrote,

The world does not consist of
100 percent Christians and
100 percent non-Christians.
There are people (a great many
of them) who are slowly ceasing
to be Christians but who still call
themselves by that name: some of
them are clergymen. There are other
people who are slowly becoming
Christians though they do not yet
call themselves so. . . . It is some
use comparing cats and dogs . . . in
the mass, because there one knows
definitely which is which. Also, an
animal does not turn (either slowly
or suddenly) from a dog into a cat.[14]

But human beings are in the process
of "turning into" something—something

wonderful or something wicked—all the time. From God's perspective, of course, there is no ambiguity about human destiny. He gives the great promises of being justified and sealed in the Spirit to encourage all who would follow Jesus that this is not ultimately a human enterprise.

When people define *Christian* in terms of having satisfied the minimum entrance requirements for getting into heaven, it always leads to "where to set the bar" debates. Some people set a high bar, saying that only a few radically obedient followers will get into heaven. People who take such a position are thought of as either champions of radical commitment or as exclusionary or legalistic, depending on whether you agree with them.

Others will set a "low bar" for getting into heaven. They are thought of as champions of grace or as lax about sin or soft on doctrine, depending on whether or not you agree with them.

But Jesus is radically gracious in his desire to accept and love, and he is radically silent about the minimum amount a borderline person needs to believe or do to get into heaven when they die.

The bar Jesus sets for discipleship is not arbitrary. Someone who genuinely wants it above all else will do whatever it takes and consider it a bargain. So it is with a disciple who wants to live in the Kingdom of God. They will follow Jesus. Their life is centered around him.

That is why, when it comes to the question of who is in with God and who is out, Jesus and the New Testament consistently focus on the center, not on the boundaries.

There is an old tradition on large Australian ranches located on often-dry land that there are two ways of keeping cattle on the ranch. One is to build a fence; the other is to dig a well.

What a gift it might be to a world that has become increasingly polarized and politicized if the church would be utterly committed to Jesus as our center. No fences to keep others out, just the life-giving water of Jesus, drawing people ever closer to his presence.

## Is It Possible to Lose My Salvation?

People sometimes wonder, "Can I lose my salvation?"

Of course, what most people are really asking is, "Is it possible that if I were to die on Monday I would go to heaven and be with God, but if I were to die on Wednesday after some spiritual backsliding that I would go to hell?" In other words, "Is it possible—at one point in my life—to be in the 'heaven-bound' category but then get shifted into the 'hell-bound' category?"

The short answer is no. You can lose your car keys or your wallet or your way home, but not this.

Salvation is an interactive relationship with God, whereby we receive forgiveness by grace and learn to surrender our will to God's so that we are living in his Kingdom together with him. It's not fire insurance. We cannot "lose" it, but we *can* reject it.

"Losing" an object is something we do unintentionally. It happens by mistake or through carelessness. A relationship with God is not something that God will allow to be "lost" in that way.

Dallas Willard put it like this:

We should be very sure that the ruined soul is not one who has missed a few more or less important theological points and will flunk a theological examination at the end of life. Hell is not an "oops!" or a slip. One does not miss heaven by a hair, but by constant effort to avoid and escape God. "Outer darkness" is for one who, everything said, wants it, whose entire orientation has slowly and firmly set itself against God and therefore against how the universe actually is.[15]

The Bible itself is full of assurance that nothing can "separate us from the love of God that is in Christ Jesus our Lord" (Romans 8:39). Jesus promises that to whomever he gives eternal life, "no one can snatch them out of my hand" (John 10:28).

However, the Bible also warns us that it's possible for a human being to reject God: "If we deliberately keep on sinning after we have received the knowledge of the truth, no sacrifice for sins is left, but only a fearful expectation of judgment" (Hebrews 10:26-27).

We are not called to spiritual anxiety. Nor are we called to spiritual complacency.

Our confidence is to be found not in some formula or arrangement that once agreed to can never be broken even if I desperately want to break it, but rather in an ongoing and ever-deepening interactive participation in the reality of the Kingdom.

Often when people ask, "How can I know I'm saved?" they are offered checklists:

Did you confess that Jesus is Lord?
Did you trust him—not just with
    intellectual assent but with a
    willingness to give him your life?
Did you sincerely repent?

If you've done these things, then you can know you are saved.

The problem for any thoughtful person, however, is the ambiguity of the checklist itself. *How "willing" do I have to be? How much certainty does trust require? Seventy percent? Ninety percent?* None of us can offer perfect certainty or perfect willingness. Not only that, our sense of certainty often fluctuates. *What if I was ninety percent certain then but only fifty percent certain now? Does my past certainty override my present doubt?*

The deeper issue behind all these problems is that we're asking the wrong question. The question is not "Am I 'saved'?" The question is "Am I following Jesus?" And I follow Jesus not so that I can get into heaven but because following Jesus is the greatest offer ever given to the human race.

## If God Loves Us So Much, Why Doesn't He Just Let Everyone into Heaven?

Good question.

Now I've got one for you.

How do you define *heaven*?

Most human beings believe in an afterlife, and in most cases, there's a good place and a bad place. If you're a good person, and you embrace the right beliefs, you go to the good place. If you're not, and you don't, you go to the bad place. Seems simple enough.

In Christian circles, the good place is heaven, and many if not most Christians think of heaven as an eternal pleasure factory of sorts, where you are always happy, you have amazing superpowers, and you can eat, drink, and do whatever you want free from guilt, fear, or consequences. Simply put, in most people's eyes, heaven is the kind of place where anybody would *love* to spend eternity—provided they're allowed in, that is.

In fact, people often criticize Christianity because it portrays heaven as an exclusive club that everyone desperately wants to get into and that they believe God is trying to keep people out of.

The reality that Jesus taught, however, is that no one really *wants* heaven.

Why? Because heaven—as Jesus describes it—is simply (and amazingly) life with God.

In fact, in heaven, it will be impossible to avoid God. It's not as if heaven is an immense place, and you have to track God down somewhere like he's the Wizard of Oz. Heaven does not contain God; God contains heaven. So becoming the kind of person who *wants* heaven—uninterrupted life with God—is a problem because I often want freedom to do things I don't want God to see. Real heaven means life where my every thought, deed, and word lie ceaselessly open to God. For eternity.

Think about it. Have you ever committed a sexual sin? I'll bet you didn't do it while your mother was watching you. That would have taken all the fun out of it. In order to commit a sin and enjoy it, you have to be someplace your mother isn't. In heaven, there is no place where God is not. Once you're in heaven, there is no little "sin" room to run to for a quick smoke. If you want to gossip, hoard, judge, self-promote, overindulge, or be cynical, where will you go?

My friend Dallas Willard once said, "I am thoroughly convinced that God will let everyone into heaven who, in his considered opinion, can stand it."[16]

The problem is, "standing it" may be more difficult than we imagine—especially those of us hoping for the eternal pleasure factory. That is why C. S. Lewis writes that "the doors of hell are locked on the *inside*."[17] Hell, whatever else it may be, is the absence of God. And more people want that than you might think.

In other words, heaven is the kind of place where people who want to sin would be miserable.

A nonsmoking restaurant is great if you're a nonsmoker but miserable to a nicotine addict. What brings joy to one creature may torture another. As C. S. Lewis once wrote, "A heaven for mosquitoes and a hell for men could very conveniently be combined."[18]

I suspect that's why they say there is a stairway to heaven but a highway to hell.

There is an old song, "Rock of Ages," that has a wonderful line:

*Be of sin the double cure;*
*Save from wrath and make me pure.*

We all want the "saved from wrath" part of the cure. God was so willing to save us from wrath that he sent Jesus to the cross to experience ultimate spiritual death in our place. That's great. The tricky part is "make me pure."

Our issue with heaven is not so much about getting in; it's about becoming the kind of person for whom heaven would be an appropriate and welcome setting. If I don't want the unceasing presence of God in my life now, how could I truly want an eternity in the ceaseless presence of God, where the possibility of any sinful action or thought— no matter how desirable—is forever cut off?

This is why Christians have always insisted that there is something worse than suffering, and that something is evil. Evil is to will the bad. It is worse than suffering because suffering is something that happens *to* you; evil is something that happens *in* you. It is twisted thinking and corrupt desire and envy and arrogance enthroned.

That's why we need to shift our thinking on salvation.

Remember, salvation isn't about you getting into heaven; it's about heaven getting into you.

---

## What about Babies and People Who Have Never Heard about God? Can They Be Saved?

People often wonder about the eternal destiny of those who may never have the opportunity to know about Jesus—babies, for instance, or people who live in parts of the world where they do not know Jesus' story.

The reason this question cannot be directly answered is that it asks, "What's the minimum amount of correct doctrine someone has to believe in order to be allowed into heaven when they die? How certain do they have to be about the Incarnation? What theory of the Atonement do they have to affirm before God will let them in?"

We don't know the answer to that question—and for good reason. The goal of the biblical writers was to get their readers to obey the call to follow Christ, not to speculate on the fate of those who do not know his story.

Now, we do know that Paul says people have "clearly seen" the invisible qualities of God from creation itself (see Romans 1:20). And we know that Paul told the Athenians who had been ignorant about much of God's identity and nature, "In the past God overlooked such ignorance, but now he commands all people everywhere to repent" (Acts 17:30).

The good news is that God will certainly allow everyone into heaven who can possibly stand it. As we have already discussed, however, "standing it" may be a good deal harder than we think.

Jesus instructed his followers with great urgency to "go and make disciples of all nations" (Matthew 28:19). This urgency was not so much because he was worried that people might go to a "bad place" but rather that they might become bad people. Remember, the worst fate in Scripture is not pain; it is evil. Pain is something that happens *to* you; evil is something that happens *in* you. It twists your mind and thoughts and desires and intentions until you become enslaved to it.

Discipleship to the gracious and forgiving carpenter from Nazareth is the sure path out of such a fate. All who follow him urgently desire to help others do the same—not because they worry about God being churlish or exclusionary but because the capacity of human beings to be deceived about our own captivity to the "Kingdom of Self" is endless.

## Why Does All of This Matter?

Because your salvation is about much more than *your* salvation.

The salvation of any individual is meaningful only as part of God's ultimate plan to save and heal all of creation.

In other words, my salvation becomes meaningful only insofar as I die to the outcomes of my own life and seek to be useful to God in the service of others.

"Saving faith" is not just good news for the one who has it. It's good news for the poor; it's good news for orphans and widows; it's good news for the trafficked; it's good news for the bullied; it's good news for the hungry; it's good news for the refugee.

Saving faith is what makes people say, "Here's my time; I'll serve"; "Here's my money; I'll give"; "Here's my life; I'll care."

Because having a loving Father watching

over them and over every member of the human race has gone from a creed they profess to their mental map of the way things are. They believe in it the way they believe in gravity. And it doesn't just save *them*; it starts becoming a part of God's project to save the world.

Like a lot of Christians, I grew up praying the "Beam me up, Scotty" prayer from the old Star Trek series. I thought we were supposed to ask God to get us out of this messed-up earth so we could go to heaven.

But Jesus did not teach the "Beam me up" prayer. He said we are to pray, "Your kingdom come, your will be done, on earth as it is in heaven" (Matthew 6:10). In other words, not "Get me out of down here so I can go up there," but "Make up there come down here."

Jesus told us to ask God to bring heaven—"your kingdom," "your will"—down here to my office, my neighborhood, my small group, my family, my country. Starting with my life, my body, my little kingdom. Righteousness, peace, and joy. Freedom from anxious thoughts. Serenity. The gift of identity. Not sometime in the future but right here, right now.

Bringing "up there down here" is God's project. Jesus himself—through his incarnation—is literally "up there" coming "down here."

Revelation 7:10 says, "Salvation belongs to our God," and one day, he will complete it.

The promise of the Bible is not that in eternity we will be disembodied spirits living in a cloud-furnished, pearly-gated, gold-bricked spiritual retirement community. The promise is that resurrection will come, and God's creation will be made glorious.

And so we wait. But waiting does not mean inactivity. We are called to be engaged. We are called to become a part of God's project. Because every time we bring a slice of this up-there life down here, the Kingdom of God breaks into this world.

Every time you are in conflict with someone—when you want to hurt them, gossip about them, avoid them—but instead you go to them and seek reconciliation and forgiveness, God's Kingdom is breaking into this world.

Every time you have a chunk of money and you decide to give sacrificially to some-body who is hungry or homeless or poor, God's Kingdom is breaking into the world.

Every time somebody who has an addic-tion wants to partner with God so badly that they're willing to stop hiding, acknowledge the truth, and get help from a loving com-munity, God's Kingdom is breaking into the world.

Every time a workaholic parent decides to stop idolizing their job and rearranges their life to begin to love and care for the little children entrusted to them, God's Kingdom is breaking into the world.

The Good News is not that we're called to do these things on our own, as though we're being given a longer to-do list. The Good News is that a power has become available to increasingly turn us into the kind of people who naturally and recreationally do such things.

That's why when Jesus goes to Zacchaeus's house and Zacchaeus gives half his possessions to the poor and agrees to pay back all he has cheated four times over, Jesus says, "Today salvation has come to this house" (Luke 19:9).

That doesn't just mean that Zacchaeus will be with God when he dies (although of course he will). It means Jesus has come to this house—that up there is coming down here, because now—through Jesus—a corrupt tax collector has become a Kingdom bringer, the poor are being helped, the cheated are receiving justice, and God's will is being done on earth as it is in heaven.

This is what the gospel does: it makes up there come down here. Beginning with you and me.

This is why it's so important that we understand what salvation really means, and why this topic matters so desperately to our lives.

But it's not just that. If we view salvation as "making the cut," it violates the Great Commandment to love God by making God look unlovable and exclusive. It leads people to wonder, *Why* doesn't *God let more people in?*

If we view salvation simply as "making the cut," it violates the great commission. Jesus told us to make disciples. But if we teach a salvation message that is solely about getting in, we are proclaiming a salvation that is disconnected from actually becoming a disciple of Jesus. And the tragic result is millions of people who live needlessly untouched by the presence of God.

If we view salvation wrongly, it inevitably creates a warped sense of us vs. them with those who haven't made the cut. It keeps people outside from coming in. It keeps people inside from changing. And it keeps up there from coming down here.

One more thing. If we view salvation wrongly, we miss the whole point of what was perhaps the most significant event in human history . . .

## If Salvation Means Living as Jesus Did in Daily Communion with God, Then Why Did He Have to Die on the Cross?

We've talked about heaven, eternal life, saving grace, and what it means to be a follower of Christ, but it is impossible to truly understand salvation without looking at the story of the Cross.

If you are familiar with the Bible, you may have noticed that the Old Testament was a pretty rough time to be an animal. Animals got slaughtered on a regular basis; their blood was sprinkled on the furniture, their fat was burned on the altar—all manner of things happened back then that PETA would never stand for, because it was believed that doing these things made human beings right with God.

In fact, if you read the Old Testament, you'll notice people were offering animal sacrifices well before Moses gave any instructions about them. It was simply a way of life. Even in ancient times, people seemed to understand that human beings were not in control of everything. What's more, they couldn't help but notice that life often comes out of death (e.g., "Animals die and plants are harvested so that I can eat and survive"), and there was something sacred about this. Thus, meals were not treated as purely secular events but rather as sacrifices to the gods.

In the ancient world, sacrifice wasn't about losing something; it was about transferring something. It was about moving something from the human/ordinary/common realm to the divine realm.

That's why references to animal sacrifices appear dozens of times throughout the Old Testament, as in these examples:

> As an aroma pleasing to the LORD,
> offer a burnt offering.
> NUMBERS 29:2

> It was a burnt offering, a pleasing
> aroma, a food offering presented to
> the LORD.
> LEVITICUS 8:21

The idea was that the aroma would rise to heaven, and whatever was being sacrificed would officially belong to God.

Here's the amazing thing. God took this already-existing, universal practice of animal sacrifice and dramatically changed it to teach people three things:

- That there is only one all-loving, supremely good God,
- That human beings were not created because God needed someone to feed but because God wanted someone to love, and
- That there is something terribly and inherently wrong with the world, and that thing is—wait for it—us.

We need to be forgiven.

We need to be healed. We need to be corrected, and loved, and brought out of shame, and grown, and guided, and empowered, and remastered.

And we can't do this by ourselves. We need help.

So God himself came to earth in Jesus. He was the great sacrifice that allowed us to move from the human/ordinary/common realm to the divine one.

In Jesus, a new kind of power had been unleashed. Not the power of force; the power of self-sacrificing love.

Turn the other cheek.

Go the second mile.

Forgive seventy times seven.

He defeated the power of evil and hate by showing that the power of self-sacrificing love is stronger. Here is what the apostle Paul wrote about this:

> [God] forgave us all our sins, having canceled the charge of our legal

indebtedness, which stood against
us and condemned us; he has taken
it away, nailing it to the cross.
And having disarmed the powers
and authorities, he made a public
spectacle of them, triumphing over
them by the cross.
COLOSSIANS 2:13-15

The powers that be thought they stripped
Jesus, defeated Jesus, made a public spectacle of Jesus, and triumphed over Jesus by the
cross. But Paul says it was exactly the oppo-
site. It was *Jesus* defeating *them*.

But it's *how* he defeated them that
changed the world.

Through his ability to endure suffering
with holy and forgiving love, Jesus defeated
the capacity of evil and hatred and sin to
inflict suffering. He showed up evil and sin
and hatred for the stupid, petty, small-minded

forces they are. He stripped them of all their power to entice and to frighten.

It was as if Jesus were saying, "Come on, hate—do your worst. Come on, fear—do your worst. Come on, sin—do your worst. I will not stop loving. I will not stop caring. My capacity to absorb suffering is stronger than your capacity to inflict it."

Jesus took the worst upon himself to set us free from it. And he did it by the cross.

This is also significant. A cross was Rome's ultimate expression of humiliation. Only slaves or traitors could be crucified. The cross was Rome's ultimate claim of superiority and triumph over a failed Messiah. The cross was as low as you could go.

That's why Jesus had to die on a cross.

Not in the sense that God wouldn't have been allowed to forgive us otherwise. God can forgive however he wants.

Jesus descended as low as you could go.

He defanged the cross.

He transformed the cross.

He turned everything upside down at the cross, because the cross declares that evil at its worst is no match for God at his best.

And yet our response to the cross is often to misunderstand it. People tend to think, *Jesus died so I don't have to.* But what they should be thinking—what we all must realize—is that *Jesus was crucified so I could be crucified with him.*

Richard Hays wrote, "The gospel story is not just the story of a super-hero who once upon a time defeated the cosmic villains of Law, Sin, and Death and thus discharged us from all responsibility; it is also the enactment of a life-pattern into which we are drawn. This is why Paul can say, 'I have been crucified with Christ.'"[19]

There is deeply embedded in the universe what might be called the "Law of Sacrifice."

A mother sacrifices her body, and her comfort, and her time so that a child can be born. A seed goes into the ground and dies so that grain can live. People who have a cause they are willing to die for have a reason to live.

The question is not whether you will offer yourself as a sacrifice; the question is what will you offer yourself as a sacrifice for?

> Therefore, I urge you brothers and
> sisters, in view of God's mercy,
> to present your bodies as a living
> sacrifice, holy and pleasing to God.
> ROMANS 12:1

Remember, a sacrifice isn't where something gets lost. A sacrifice is where something gets transferred.

Follow God's example, therefore, as dearly loved children and walk in

the way of love, just as Christ loved
us and gave himself up for us as a
fragrant offering and sacrifice to God.
EPHESIANS 5:1-2

For we are to God the pleasing aroma
of Christ.
2 CORINTHIANS 2:15

Some people think that if they believe
the right things about what happened on the
cross, they get to go to heaven when they die.
But that's not how Jesus' first followers saw
it. They saw something more. They saw it
as the beginning of God's great plan to save
his world. They saw it as an invitation to
become a people of the Cross, to join Jesus
in the power of self-sacrificing love. In the
wonderful words of N. T. Wright, "They saw
it as the day the revolution began."[20]

A lot of people think the only real reason

Jesus came to earth was to die on the cross. But death on the cross was only one part of his mission. His overall mission was to be the Kingdom bringer.

His one gospel was the gospel of the availability of the Kingdom.

His one purpose was to model the reality of that Kingdom in his life, death, and resurrection.

His one command was to pursue the Kingdom.

His one plan was for his people to extend the Kingdom.

He invites you, as a gracious gift, to become an agent of the Kingdom—to experience God's reign in your own life, body, and will and then to become a conduit of God's power, joy, and love to a bruised and bleeding humanity all around you.

The gospel of Jesus' Kingdom offers the salvation of despairing individuals and the healing of systemic injustice. It is the hope of the world.

I have a book on my shelf with the intriguing title *What's the Least I Can Believe and Still Be a Christian?*

In a chapter on the Resurrection, the author recalls a scene from the Tom Hanks movie *Cast Away*.[21] Tom Hanks's character, Noland, is going to get married to his dream girl, but his plane goes down in the middle of the ocean, and he is marooned on an island for years. Noland is a FedEx executive, and a number of packages wash ashore with him. He finds great uses for them all.

But one package, the last package, Noland does not open. Whatever its contents, they will remain unknown and unused.

Four years later, Noland builds a raft and lashes himself and that package to it. Against all odds, he survives and makes it home.

He is saved.

In the final scene of the movie, he delivers the package to its rightful owner, but the owner is not home. So Noland leaves a note: "This package saved my life."

What does he mean by "saved"? Other packages had contents far more useful—things he could use to cut or tie or build. This one remained a mystery.

This package was hope.

Every time he looked at it, he was reminded of his job, his vocation. Every time he looked at it, he remembered that he might yet get off the island. Every time he looked at it, he knew there was a larger world than his little prison.

Hope keeps you going when nothing else will.

"This package saved my life."

I don't know the least you can believe and still be a Christian. Only God knows that.

I know that if he was willing to come to

earth and die on a cross, he's more eager than I am to save anybody who can stand it.

I know the Good Place that such a God would envision must be beyond my capacity to imagine. I know that the person that I am to become when I "shall be like him" (1 John 3:2)—like Adam II—exceeds my wildest dreams for myself.

"Help is on the way."

This is the message in a bottle of the strange book called the Bible.

"Help is on the way."

This is the announcement of the unique man, Jesus. Here and there, this message washes up again on the shore of one I-land or another.

"Help is on the way."

This is the package called hope.

And hope—if it is placed in the right object—can save your life. Which brings us back to our first question.

## How Do I Know If I'm Really Saved?

Often people in Christian circles will answer this question with a little checklist to make sure you trusted in some arrangement to get into heaven: Did you really believe? Did you pray the right prayer? Did you fully surrender?

The problem with this is we are not called to trust an arrangement. We are called to trust the Arranger.

Confidence in our salvation is only one indivisible part of a larger confidence: confidence in God, for today as well as eternity. I can only trust him with my eternity to the extent that I'm actually trusting him with my now. Trust is a by-product of knowing. As I come to know God through interactive engagement, I come to know that he is the kind of person who will do his best eternally for every person he has made.

Including me.
How can I know if I'm really saved?
Know God.

# GLOSSARY OF FREQUENTLY MISUNDERSTOOD TERMS

**Gospel (often misunderstood):** The minimum entrance requirements for getting into heaven when you die.

**Gospel (as Jesus proclaimed it):** The announcement of the availability of life in the Kingdom of God through Jesus himself (see Mark 1:14-15; Matthew 4:17; 6:33).

**Disciple (often misunderstood):** A Christian who is doing spiritual extra-credit work.

**Disciple (more correctly):** Someone whose ultimate goal is to live the way Jesus would live if Jesus were in their shoes.

**Christian (often misunderstood):** Someone who believes the essential tenets of Christianity required to get into heaven after death.

**Christian (more correctly):** Another word for disciple (used only three times in the New Testament—always of the community of disciples).

**Eternal Life (often misunderstood):** Going to heaven when you die.

**Eternal Life (more correctly):** An interactive, participative relationship with God that begins now and which death is powerless to stop. ("This is eternal life: that they know you, the only true God, and Jesus Christ, whom you have sent" John 17:3.)

**Grace (often misunderstood):** The free forgiveness of sins.

**Grace (more correctly):** God at work in us to do what we cannot do on our own. This includes forgiveness but also includes much more. Peter says we are to "grow in grace"; he doesn't mean "grow in the forgiveness of your sins." God was gracious before anyone sinned. We are meant to live by grace.

**Salvation (often misunderstood):** Having satisfied the minimum requirements for being in the "heaven-bound" category.

**Salvation (more correctly):** The past, present, and future journey of being delivered from sin for a life with God.

**Faith (often misunderstood):** Things you're supposed to believe about God.

**Faith (more correctly):** Your "mental map" about how things are.

**Saving Faith (often misunderstood):** The least you have to believe in order to get into heaven when you die.

**Saving Faith (more correctly):** The "mental map" of reality that has the tendency toward natural obedience to Jesus.

**Heaven (often misunderstood):** The divine pleasure factory where anyone would be happy if they could just get in.

**Heaven (in its afterlife dimensions, more correctly):** The redeemed new creation in which God will be impossible to avoid.

**Trusting Christ (often misunderstood):** Believing that affirming a certain doctrine means I cannot be kept out of heaven when I die.

**Trusting Christ (more correctly):** Believing Jesus was right—about everything—and therefore seeking intelligently to obey him.

# KEY VERSES
# ABOUT SALVATION

FROM THE NEW LIVING TRANSLATION

This is the way to have eternal life—
to know you, the only true God,
and Jesus Christ, the one you sent to
earth.

JOHN 17:3

Everyone who has given up houses or
brothers or sisters or father or mother
or children or property, for my sake,
will receive a hundred times as much
in return and will inherit eternal life.

MATTHEW 19:29

You search the Scriptures because
you think they give you eternal
life. But the Scriptures point to
me [Jesus]!
JOHN 5:39

The Spirit alone gives eternal life.
Human effort accomplishes nothing.
JOHN 6:63

Just as sin ruled over all people and
brought them to death, now God's
wonderful grace rules instead, giving
us right standing with God and
resulting in eternal life through Jesus
Christ our Lord.
ROMANS 5:21

This is how God loved the world: He gave his one and only Son, so that everyone who believes in him will not perish but have eternal life.

JOHN 3:16

---

The wages of sin is death, but the free gift of God is eternal life through Christ Jesus our Lord.

ROMANS 6:23

Anyone who believes in God's Son has eternal life. Anyone who doesn't obey the Son will never experience eternal life but remains under God's angry judgment.

JOHN 3:36

I tell you the truth, those who listen
to my message and believe in God
who sent me have eternal life. They
will never be condemned for their
sins, but they have already passed
from death into life.

JOHN 5:24


I trust in you for salvation, O LORD!

GENESIS 49:18


The LORD is my light and my
      salvation—
  so why should I be afraid?
The LORD is my fortress, protecting me
      from danger,
  so why should I tremble?

PSALM 27:1

He alone is my rock and my
salvation, my fortress where I will
never be shaken.
PSALM 62:2

What makes us think we can escape
if we ignore this great salvation that
was first announced by the Lord
Jesus himself and then delivered to us
by those who heard him speak?
HEBREWS 2:3

Salvation is not a reward for the good
things we have done, so none of us
can boast about it.
EPHESIANS 2:9

# NOTES

1. Dallas Willard, *The Spirit of the Disciplines: Understanding How God Changes Lives* (New York: HarperSanFrancisco, 1988), 32.
2. Frank C. Laubach, *Man of Prayer: Selected Writings of a World Missionary* (Syracuse, NY: Laubach Literacy International, 1990), 195.
3. Brother Lawrence, *The Practice of the Presence of God* (New Kensington, PA: Whitaker House, 1982), 82.
4. Dallas Willard, *The Great Omission: Reclaiming Jesus's Essential Teachings on Discipleship* (New York: HarperSanFrancisco, 2006), 166.
5. Alcoholics Anonymous, *Twelve Steps and Twelve Traditions* (New York: The A. A. Grapevine and Alcoholics Anonymous World Services, 1981), 106–7.
6. Michael Burkhimer, *Lincoln's Christianity* (Yardley, PA: Westholme, 2007), xi.
7. Willard, *The Spirit of the Disciplines*, 258.
8. Dietrich Bonhoeffer, *The Cost of Discipleship* (New York: Touchstone, 1959), 51.

9. Simon Sinek, "How Great Leaders Inspire Action," filmed September 2009, at TEDxPugetSound, video, 17:58, https://www.ted.com/talks/simon_sinek_how _great_leaders_inspire_action.

10. Bonhoeffer, *The Cost of Discipleship*, 46, 56.

11. Helen Keller, *The Story of My Life*, ed. John Albert Macy (New York: Grosset and Dunlap, 1905), 23–24.

12. Thomas Merton, *Contemplative Prayer*, (New York: Image Books, 1969), 13.

13. Tim Harmon, "Who's In and Who's Out? Christianity and Bounded Sets vs. Centered Sets," *Transformed* (blog), January 17, 2014, https://www .westernseminary.edu/transformedblog/2014/01/17 /whos-in-and-whos-out-christianity-and-bounded -sets-vs-centered-sets/.

14. C. S. Lewis, *Mere Christianity* (New York: HarperCollins, 1980), 209–10.

15. Dallas Willard, *Renovation of the Heart: Putting on the Character of Christ* (Colorado Springs: NavPress, 2002), 59.

16. Dallas Willard, *The Divine Conspiracy: Rediscovering Our Hidden Life in God* (New York: HarperSanFrancisco, 1998), 302.

17. C. S. Lewis, *The Problem of Pain* (New York: HarperOne, 2001), 130.

18. Ibid., 141.

19. Richard B. Hays, *The Faith of Jesus Christ: The Narrative Substructure of Galatians 3:1–4:11* (Grand Rapids, MI: Eerdmans, 2002), 211.

20. N. T. Wright, *The Day the Revolution Began: Reconsidering the Meaning of Jesus's Crucifixion* (New York: HarperOne, 2016), 4.

21. Martin Thielen, *What's the Least I Can Believe and Still Be a Christian? A Guide to What Matters Most* (Louisville, KY: John Knox Press, 2013), 116–17.

# ABOUT THE AUTHOR

**John Ortberg** is an author, a speaker, and the senior pastor of Menlo Church in the San Francisco Bay Area. A consistent theme of John's teaching is how to follow a Jesus way of life—that is, how faith in Christ can affect our everyday lives with God. His books include *All the Places to Go . . . How Will You Know?*; *Soul Keeping*; *Who Is This Man?*; *The Life You've Always Wanted*; *Faith and Doubt*; and *If You Want to Walk on Water, You've Got to Get Out of the Boat*. John teaches around the world at conferences and churches.

Born and raised in Rockford, Illinois,

John graduated from Wheaton College. He holds a master's of divinity and a doctorate in clinical psychology from Fuller Seminary, and he did postgraduate work at the University of Aberdeen, Scotland.

John is a member of the board of trustees at Fuller Seminary, where he has also served as an adjunct faculty member. He is on the board of the Dallas Willard Center for Christian Spiritual Formation and has served in the past on the board of Christianity Today International.

Now that their children are grown, John and his wife, Nancy, enjoy surfing in the Pacific to help care for their souls. He can be followed on Twitter @johnortberg.

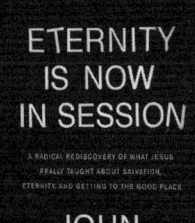